Original title:
The Spirit of Giving

Copyright © 2024 Creative Arts Management OÜ
All rights reserved.

Author: Rafael Sterling
ISBN HARDBACK: 978-9916-94-056-3
ISBN PAPERBACK: 978-9916-94-057-0

Embraced by Kindness

In a world of cookies, sweet and round,
Gifts of laughter are always found.
A jolly old chap with a red-nosed grin,
Spreads joy and cheer, let the fun begin!

Wrapped up in laughter, a dance of delight,
Socks for the cat, what a funny sight!
Unexpected surprises, oh what a thrill,
A rubber chicken, and the room's laughter spills.

Silly hats piled high, a costume parade,
Frogs wearing scarves, how this joy cascades!
In the gift of a smile, we share our heart,
Even if it's just a kin's weird art.

Hand in hand we frolic, our spirits are bright,
With giggles and chuckles, our friendship takes flight.
In this wonderland we create each day,
The best gifts are those that make us say,

'This is the moment, full of surprise,'
With a wink and a laugh, happiness flies!
So here's to the fun, wrapped in a bow,
In the joy of giving, watch the laughter grow!

Sharing Beneath the Stars

In the dark, a sandwich flies,
A lunch for two, oh what a surprise!
I flung it high, it hit the moon,
Now aliens feast and hum a tune.

Beneath the stars, we laugh and play,
Juggling donuts on a bright display.
A cookie lands atop my head,
As friends all giggle and laugh instead.

Embracing Abundance

In a thrift shop, I found a hat,
With feathers bright, and oh so fat!
Wore it proud as I strolled outside,
Gave it away, it had such pride!

A neighbor's dog once stole my shoe,
I chased him down, but what to do?
Gave him a treat and shared my grin,
Now we swap shoes, let the fun begin!

Acts of Silent Love

A note left wedged in a table crack,
Said, 'I borrowed your pen, but I'll bring it back!'
Unbeknownst to me, it was a prank,
My friend had swapped it with a skank!

Silent love in funny ways,
Like stealing cookies on rainy days.
Baked a pie, but it turned out flat,
So I gifted it to the neighborhood cat!

Whispers of Charity

In my pocket, a jingle and clank,
I thought to give, but all I had was a prank.
Put a rubber chicken in the hat,
And laughed when folks took a swing at that!

Whispers stirred, as joy took flight,
A dance-off broke out, what a sight!
As laughter echoed far and wide,
We charmed the world, all smiles applied!

Windows of the Soul

Eyes wide as saucers, hungry for fun,
Glimmers of kindness shine bright like the sun.
A cookie for a smile, a giggle exchanged,
We're hoarding our joy, like kids so deranged.

Giggles and snorts, a chorus of cheer,
Sharing our odd socks, spreading the weird.
Laughter's a treasure, more precious than gold,
Let's give it away and watch joy unfold.

The Sowing of Love

Plant seeds of silliness in a garden so wild,
Water with laughter, just like a child.
Fertilize with giggles, watch blossoms arise,
Surprises in the dirt, hidden like a prize.

Each joke that we share, a sprinkle of grace,
A pie in the face, makes for happy face.
Grow hugs like flowers, spread joy all around,
In this wacky farm, pure bliss can be found.

Seasons of Care

Winter brings snowballs, warm mittens to toss,
Catch laughs like snowflakes, oh what a loss!
Spring brings the pranks, oh it's time to play,
A dance in the rain, let's squawk and sway.

Summer sizzles with ice cream galore,
We'll share a big cone, then waddle for more.
Fall brings the pumpkins, round and bright,
We'll carve silly faces, spreading delight!

The Harmony of Giving

In a band of chuckles, we strum our delight,
Playing heartstrings with laughter so bright.
A symphony of smiles, what a splendid show,
Let's dance through the day, let silliness flow.

With spoons made of giggles and forks forged in fun,
We'll feast on the joy until the day's done.
Harmony in laughter, a chorus we'll sing,
Who knew joy and mischief could make such a sting?

Lanterns in the Night

In a field of lanterns, we decide to share,
The glow of friendship hangs in the air.
We trip on a pumpkin, let out a yelp,
Turning grumbles to giggles, it's hard to help.

Socks stuffed with donuts, we pass them around,
It's a tasty explosion, our laughter's profound.
Each light that we hold, sways with delight,
In this whimsical dance, we're stars of the night.

A Tapestry of Grace

With mismatched mittens, we weave a warm quilt,
Stitching in kindness, with love gently built.
A croaky old parrot steals cookies and fun,
As we roll on the floor, our giggles just run.

Lace up your sneakers, let's chase down the breeze,
Each step's an adventure, a great way to please.
With taffy and laughter, our pockets get filled,
A patchwork of joy, in harmony thrilled.

The Warmth of Shared Smiles

Underneath a tree, we start up a game,
Tossing around jokes, nothing's the same.
A squirrel drops a acorn, on someone's bright head,
And all of us burst, our smiles widely spread.

In the circle of laughter, we share silly tales,
Of goats in tutus and dancing snails.
With each silly story, we sprinkle some cheer,
Found in the moments when friends gather near.

Cocoa and Kindness

Hot cocoa's steaming, we gather in line,
With whipped cream mustaches, we're feeling divine.
A marshmallow mischief makes cocoa go splat,
As we giggle and snort, it's a riot, just that!

We mix in some sprinkles, add humor with glee,
Each sip is a wink, each laugh is a spree.
In this cozy circle, where sweetness unfolds,
We sip on our sunshine, as laughter retolds.

Embracing the Unseen

In a world full of snacks, we toss and we cheer,
The joy of a gift makes our worries unclear.
With a wink and a grin, we hand out some pies,
While secretly hoping for no messy flies.

A cat in a box makes the neighbors all stare,
We'll share our old clothes while dancing in air.
A sock for a hat, let the madness ensue,
This spirit of fun brings us closer, it's true.

The Bridge of Giving

With smiles as wide as our favorite beach,
We gather our laughter, it's within our reach.
Sharing old jokes like they're freshly baked goods,
Hoping they land just as well as they should.

A plumber with cookies brings hope to the fray,
While squirrels on skateboards steal snacks on the way.
As we bridge every gap with some silly delight,
These moments of sharing turn wrongs into right.

Mosaics of Joy

A patchwork of laughter, our hearts in a spin,
We throw in some giggles, sprinkle the grin.
Each funny gesture, like a clown on the stage,
Creates a mosaic, no need for a gauge.

When a fruitcake appears, we all take a breath,
Is this a gift or perhaps just a jest?
With layers of humor and sprinkles of fun,
Mosaics of joy mean we all get to run.

A Symphony of Sharing

With kazoos and old socks, we start the parade,
As melodies tumble, our worries do fade.
A banjo made from a pot and a spoon,
Playing tunes that will leave us quite immune.

The orchestra laughs while they pass all the snacks,
With each silly note, we forget all the chacks.
In this symphony wild, we each play our part,
Sharing is sweet, like a tickle to the heart.

The Bond of Giving

When socks go missing, oh what a tease,
A donation bag springs up with ease.
Leftover cookies, stale but sweet,
Sharing them all, now that's a treat!

A neighbor's cat joins in on the fun,
Stealing your lunch while you just run.
But laughter echoes through the hall,
For joy in giving beats it all!

Kindness Blossoms

A smile can sprout like flowers in spring,
Even grumpy folks can join in and sing.
With each little token passed here and there,
The world gets brighter, as we all share.

Old clothes and gadgets float on by,
Turning frowns upside down, oh my!
A mismatched sock finds a new friend,
In kindness, we giggle, and they blend.

A Journey of Hearts

Packed up a sandwich, all crusts removed,
On a caper to spread joy, so much improved.
But a squirrel swooped in, oh what a sight,
He took half the bread, left the rest tight!

On a quest for laughter, we share our pies,
Who knew dessert could wear such a disguise?
With each silly mishap, together we cheer,
Unplanned adventures make memories dear!

Unfolding Generosity

A little old lady with a big heart,
Decided to bake; oh, where do we start?
Her cookies explode like confetti galore,
Whisking up giggles; who could want more?

A high-five for exchanges, a nod for some aid,
The mailman's got cookies, and ducts he delayed.
In this wild ride of sharing delight,
Laughter rings true, like stars in the night!

The Call of Altruism

When you give a toy to a cat,
It'll play with it, then nap like that.
You think it's sharing, oh what a joke,
That cat just wants to poke the smoke.

Let's bake a cake for the neighbor's dog,
He'll wag his tail and play like a hog.
But when you think you're doing good,
He'll snatch the last piece like he knew he could!

In a world where kindness should reign,
I tripped while giving away my brain.
But it's fine, it'd roll to the street,
Spreading smiles, oh what a treat!

So spread your joy like peanut butter,
Stick it around and hear the clutter.
For in the mess, you'll surely find,
Laughter's the best gift of all, combined!

The Tides of Kindness

Oh waves of kindness crash and fall,
They drag me under, yet I call.
I offer help, toss out a float,
And watch as my good deed starts to gloat.

I gave my sandwich to a bird,
It looked so hungry, not a word.
But then my lunch flew out with sass,
And I was left to nibble on grass!

Let's share our laughter, let's share our time,
But be careful of picking up a lime.
As we eat and joke, I'll spill a drink,
And down the line, we'll all just wink.

For every wave that pushes out,
Brings joy along with a silly shout.
So catch that tide and let it flow,
Kindness is what makes the giggles grow!

Gifts of Time

I wrapped my time in a shiny bow,
But friends watched me unwrap it slow.
A whole hour gone, they giggled loud,
They only wanted my snack, not the crowd.

On Tuesdays, I propose some fun,
To give an hour, not just a pun.
But as I stand to share my tips,
They just want free pizza and chips!

So here's a gift, it won't cost a dime,
Just lend me your ear, and we'll rhyme.
We'll trade our stories, it'll be prime,
As I laugh at your shoes, and you mine!

For time is funny, messy, and free,
A gift that turns glee from you to me.
So let's be silly, let laughter chime,
Sharing our moments, one silly mime!

The Language of Generosity

In a land where generosity sings,
Everyone dances, practicing their flings.
One gave a hug like it was a meal,
And others just smiled, what a surreal deal!

I heard a joke about sharing shoes,
But those weren't mine, so I had to refuse.
Yet in this game of give and take,
It seems the more you give, the more they make!

An old man offered up his gray hair,
Said it's a gift, but tangle with care.
For kindness brews a hearty stew,
Full of laughs and some bird droppings too!

So when you give, just chuckle and grin,
For joy multiplies when you let love in.
Generosity's the game we play,
Laughter's the rule—hip hip hooray!

Moments of Magic

A squirrel stole my sandwich today,
When I turned, it danced away!
With a wink and a twist, it was gone,
Leaving me laughing, all alone.

In the park, I saw kids play,
Sharing snacks in a funny way.
One dropped a donut, what a sight!
A dog rolled over, what pure delight.

A juggler tossed some old shoes high,
While pigeons below began to fly.
A crowd laughed, oh what a scene,
Laughter echoed, oh so serene.

Life's little moments, bright and sly,
Remind us all, don't be shy.
Share your goodies, lend a hand,
Magic happens—oh so grand!

The Generosity Garden

In the garden, we plant some smiles,
Water them gently, for a while.
A tomato danced with a bright green pea,
While carrots giggled, wild and free.

The flowers whispered, 'Hey, let's play!'
While bees buzzed around, hip-hip-hooray!
A pumpkin jived with a zesty lime,
Planting joy—it's our garden rhyme.

A rabbit hopped, then tripped with grace,
Fell over a radish, what a race!
Lettuce laughed, 'Not so fast!'
In this garden, fun's meant to last.

So share your harvest, share your cheer,
Magic grows with friends so dear.
In this patch of joy, we'll find,
Generosity, oh so unwind!

A River of Giving

By the river, laughter spills,
As ducks waddle and swim with skills.
A fish jumped high, splashed a friend,
Together they giggled, what a blend!

A frog croaked loud, 'Here's a treat!'
While children tossed crumbs at their feet.
A turtle peeked, with a wink in tow,
It joined the fun—oh what a show!

Floating on leaves, a party drifted,
All critters cheered, not one was gifted.
They traded jokes for a shiny stone,
In this river, silliness is sown.

So, splash around, let laughter flow,
Share a smile with all you know.
In this river of friendship, we thrive,
Making joy alive—oh what a dive!

Glimmers of Grace

In a quirky café, mugs clink and cheer,
Baristas dance, spreading love near.
A muffin tumbled, rolled on the floor,
Everyone giggled, then asked for more.

A ladybird flew through the air,
Perched on a teacup, what a dare!
Stirring sweet tea with a tiny grin,
It joined the fun, let the laughter begin.

A spoon argued with a fork all day,
'Who's the best tool?' they'd bicker and play.
But a salad came in, crisp and bright,
Declared they're all friends, what a sight!

So remember, in moments so small,
Sharing warmth can brighten us all.
In this café, glimmers ignite,
A funny tale—joy takes flight!

To Spark Joy

In the corner sat a cat,
With a hat that looked like that,
He stole my socks without a care,
Left me barefoot, oh so bare!

Then I thought, what if I share?
My mismatched socks, a fun affair!
He chased his tail in pure delight,
What a funny, joyful sight!

Grinning wide, I tossed my shoes,
He caught them fast, and much to lose,
Now my floors are free of mess,
As my wardrobe learns to bless!

So if your closet's feeling bare,
Just find a friend to show you care,
A little gift can spread the cheer,
Even if it's just some gear!

The Light Beyond

In a world where flavors fight,
Lemon pie against the night,
A pie-slice drifted off the plate,
And danced around, oh what a fate!

I chased that slice both quick and fast,
It giggled loud, it couldn't last,
Across the room, it twirled with glee,
While I just laughed, 'Oh, let it be!'

It jumped on chairs and bowed to mates,
A slice that truly delegates,
Who knew that giving pie away,
Could make you smile throughout the day?

No more leftover, my heart is light,
A joyful dance into the night,
Sometimes it's fun to lend a hand,
Or even pies, across the land!

Bowls of Charity

In a soup kitchen full of cheer,
There stood a chef with lots of beer,
He cooked up dishes, made them swell,
With laughter that rang like a bell.

"Who wants some stew?" he called out loud,
The crowd just erupted and felt so proud,
A spoon flew high, a ladle too,
These bowls of joy, oh what a view!

As someone slipped, and went for a tumble,
He got up quick, avoiding the grumble,
"Just adding spice!" he laughed with glee,
Soup for all, come taste for free!

So if you're ever feeling blue,
A bowl of soup will do for you,
Share a laugh, or just a spoon,
Who knew soup could make one swoon?

Ripple Effects

A pebble tossed in a pond so wide,
Made ripples dance, oh how they glide!
They splashed and giggled in the sun,
Who knew that stones could have such fun?

Each splash sparked laughter all around,
Every friend on the shore was found,
We threw more stones with silly grins,
And joined the party, where joy begins!

But one big splash sent us all back,
We all fell in, with quite the knack,
"What a way to make a splash!"
Together we laughed, it was quite the crash!

So share a laugh, share a cheer,
Like ripples spreading without fear,
For sometimes joy flows oh so free,
And it's best when you share it, just like me!

Threads of Connection

In a world where socks seem to flee,
I gift you one, can't you see?
With every mismatch, laughter flows,
Our friendship's bond only grows.

I wrapped my gift in bubblegum,
Your face brightens with a hum,
But beware, it's stuck to your nose,
Our giggles erupt, how it shows!

The tiny trinkets I present,
With every one, my heart is bent,
A rubber chicken may seem rude,
But hey, it's love, our weirdest food!

So here's a pen, it's out of ink,
It's the thought that counts, don't you think?
With silly gifts, our spirits rise,
Bound by laughter, no need for ties.

Hearts as Wide as Oceans

In a boat made of chocolate bars,
We sail away, past candy stars.
Your smile's the map, I cannot miss,
Together we drift in sweet bliss.

I'll trade you a rock, it's really cool,
For a laugh and a smile, that's the rule.
Our treasures are odd, but that's okay,
It's the joy in the madness we display.

With jellybeans tossed, splashes of fun,
Under the sun, our laughter's begun.
Like dolphins we dance, oh what a sight,
With hearts like the ocean, our spirits take flight.

As long as we share this silly dream,
Our friendship will always be the cream.
Cast off your worries, see how they float,
For love needs no silver—just a floaty boat!

The Currency of Love

I gave you a cookie, a sweet little treat,
You offered me gum, but it's stuck to your seat.
Our trades make us giggle, what quirk of fate,
In this shop of oddities, laughter's first rate.

A coupon for hugs, redeemable here,
You hand me a hairball, I burst out in cheer.
We barter our woes with a chuckle and grin,
For a smile's the currency where love does begin.

Each odd little token, a trinket, a prize,
Wraps bends our hearts, and opens the skies.
You gift me a frog, I can't help but croak,
In the market of joy, we've hit the right joke!

Our wallets might be empty, but spirits are rich,
With every mishap, we find our sweet niche.
So let's trade some laughter, and dance through the night,
In this bank of delight, everything feels right.

The Welcoming Hearth

At my door, there's a monster named Fred,
He's fluffy and silly, with snacks to be fed.
You laugh at his wig, it's bright pink and green,
Our hearts are warmed by this creature we've seen.

Inviting you in is a giggle-rich treat,
As we feast on the spaghetti designed as a seat.
With sauce on our noses, we chortle and cheer,
In this cozy chaos, there's nothing to fear.

I serve you croquettes shaped like a star,
You toss one at Fred, and he giggles ajar.
Each bite brings us closer, with joy we'll ignite,
This hearth full of laughter, our hearts feel so light.

So come, take a seat, pull up a chair,
With silly old Fred, there's love in the air.
In this room of delight, the wonders unwind,
The warmth of our fun is the best gift we find.

Echoes of Kindness

In a world where wallets dance,
People give a hopeful glance.
A squirrel with a tiny hat,
Shares his acorns like a brat.

A cat in boots delivers pies,
To hungry dogs who roll their eyes.
Each gift wrapped in laughter's wrap,
Brings grins wider than a map.

Balloons float up to the sky,
As dreams of joy and pies nearby.
A garden gnome with cherry roots,
Gifts out flowers in his boots.

So raise your glass, and let's toast,
To quirky kindness we love most.
For funny tales of hearts so wide,
Spark giggles in this love-filled ride.

Threads of Compassion

A grandma knits with yarn so bright,
Her kittens pounce in playful fright.
Each stitch a giggle, each purl a grin,
Her scarf for the dog makes tails spin.

A chef does magic with just one spoon,
Baking cookies that make kids swoon.
But the cat steals one, oh what a sight,
As flour flies and giggles ignite.

A clown rides by on a pogo stick,
Tossing candy and making it stick.
With each bounce, he spreads the cheer,
And turns the frown of a fussy deer.

We wrap the days in laughter's thread,
Gifts of joy where no tears are shed.
In a world where smiles connect,
We find that kindness is the best project.

Luminescent Hearts

A glowworm sings in the dark of night,
While friends bake cakes with pure delight.
Sprinkles fly like confetti streams,
As laughter echoes through their dreams.

A dog in shades struts with flair,
Delivering treats beyond compare.
He winks and barks, a clever chap,
Sharing snacks with a joyful clap.

A dance party in the park up high,
Where frogs wear shoes and birds can fly.
Each hop and leap a grateful cheer,
Spreading love from ear to ear.

So keep your heart a bright beacon,
Where giggles flow and fun is strewn.
In the dance of joy, we all play our part,
With luminescent laughter filling the heart.

The Charity Tapestry

Woven stories of quirky folk,
Share their dreams and laughter's cloak.
A bike built for two rides past,
Where kindness flies and shadows cast.

In the town square, a juggler grins,
Tossing pies where laughter begins.
He slips and trips, but hey, it's fun,
As cream pies fly under the sun.

A penguin slides down a snowy hill,
Gifting fish with a quirky thrill.
Each splash brings giggles to the shore,
As seagulls dance, wanting more.

So stitch together our hearts of gold,
With silly stories we love to hold.
In this tapestry of joy so bright,
Let humor weave our love, pure delight.

The Art of Selflessness

A hamster in a wheel, going round,
Giving gifts of fluff without a sound,
He wraps a crumb in shiny foil,
His tiny heart is free from toil.

A cat brings mice, quite the delight,
Wagging tail with all her might,
"Look what I caught, you want a bite?"
The gift is sweet, but not quite right!

A dog with bones, so big and round,
Offers them up, all stuck in the ground,
"Have a snack!" he seems to say,
While he digs up his buffet!

A goat with a sweater, knitted bright,
Gives hugs for free, oh what a sight,
But only wears it one whole day,
Then bleats, "It's mine, hey, who's in my way?"

A squirrel drops acorns, just to tease,
Playful jests with such great ease,
He hoards them all with no regret,
But shares a smile, you won't forget!

Rivers of Remembrance

In rivers flowing, gifts a glide,
With silly ducks all in a ride,
They quack and splash, what a parade,
Each feathered friend in joy displayed.

A fish jumps high, a shiny flash,
Gifts everyone a little splash,
"Want some water?" it seems to say,
While going back to play all day.

A frog on lilies with a grin,
Catches flies, throws them to a kin,
"Here's dinner, don't mind the plight,"
They dine as friends till late at night.

A turtle slow, with gifts inside,
A party hat, oh what a ride,
"Join the fun!" he shouts to all,
With laughter echoing through the hall.

A raccoon stumbles under trees,
Collects the treasures with such ease,
"Take a trinket, it's all a game,"
And leaves them laughing just the same!

Illuminating Shadows

In shadows dance the midnight crew,
With glowsticks bright, they make a hue,
A wink, a smile, they share the light,
Making the dark a bit more bright.

A ghostly friend with chains that rattle,
Offers odd snacks, it's quite the battle,
"Try my cookies, they're out of sight!"
Yet all they taste is pure moonlight.

A bat in cap, with shades to wear,
Hangs upside down, quite the flair,
"Want a crash course on how to fly?"
He'll surely tease, and then comply!

A shadow cat with purring sound,
Gifts cuddles safe, no fear around,
"Join my dream, but take good care,"
For naps can lead to quite the scare!

Together they make quite a scene,
These playful folks, they all convene,
With laughter echoing through the air,
And brighter days without a care!

Beneath the Tree of Benevolence

Beneath the tree, in laughter's shade,
A monkey swings, a grand charade,
He tosses fruit, a fruity hail,
While giggles rise, they never fail.

A parrot, bright, with jokes so loud,
Cracks 'em up, makes quite a crowd,
"Why did the banana cross the way?"
He winds up with a silly play!

A bear with honey, sticky smiles,
Offers treats from a hundred miles,
"Just a taste!" he bids with glee,
And soon enough, they all agree!

A snail in shades, oh what a trip,
Gives slow motion hugs, a gentle grip,
"Don't hurry now, enjoy the plot,"
For kindness thrives, not forgot!

Under the branches, friends all meet,
Gathering gifts that are quite sweet,
In this canopy, laughter never ends,
As joy and fun mix with good friends!

The Canvas of Humanity

With crayons bright, we laugh and share,
A doodle here, a funny scare.
Each gift a splash, a silly role,
On life's grand art, we play the soul.

A pizza slice, a joke on toes,
From grumpy cats to sawdust snows.
We paint with love, in wacky hues,
The world should giggle, not just muse.

Handshakes and giggles, what a trend,
With silly hats that never end.
On this big canvas, laughter sings,
Let's dress it up with goofy things.

So pass the joy, like jello-fling,
It's messy, bright—let's let it cling.
In every brushstroke, find a friend,
In life's wild art, we won't offend!

Beacons of Hope

We light the path with Orange Soda,
A fizzy pop, our hearts grow broader.
Each cup we raise, a chuckle high,
With sparkling smiles, we never sigh.

A chocolate bar, a wink, a grin,
Every bite's a joy, a little sin.
As laughter bubbles, like a sweet parade,
Our beacons shine, no joy betrayed.

When times are tough, we make a scene,
With rubber chickens, a quirky routine.
In funny hats, we take a stand,
Our mighty hearts, the strangest band.

So share your giggles, let them float,
Like rubber ducks, they'll surely gloat.
In this bright light, let's all partake,
With humor's warmth, the world we'll shake!

Autumn Leaves of Kindness

The leaves fall down, a rustling cheer,
While squirrels dance with autumn's beer.
A blanket tossed, all snug and bright,
Together, we create delight.

With pumpkin pies and silly hats,
We swap good jokes with all the cats.
A leaf fight here, a hug or two,
In this grand season, laughter's due.

With every step, a crunch we hear,
Silly giggles float through the sphere.
As kindness scatters like golden seeds,
Our playful hearts plant funny deeds.

So gather 'round, your pals and kin,
With goofy games, let fun begin.
In autumn's arms, let kindness show,
As laughter shines through every row!

A Quiet Generosity

A cookie shared with crumbs of joy,
A quiet act, not just for show.
We chuckle soft, in whispered glee,
While secret gifts bring harmony.

In every note, a jest to swipe,
Like sneaky ninjas, that's our type.
With shuttlecocks and giggly tales,
We float through life on friendship sails.

A wink, a nod, in passing glance,
Our silly ways invite a dance.
With every chuckle, love expands,
In this sweet quiet, life commands.

So let's embrace, in subtle laughs,
And share our hearts through playful chats.
In gentle ways, our spirits jive,
With joy and humor, we all thrive!

A Shared Meal

When food is shared, the laughter grows,
A plate of joy, as friendship flows.
The turkey trips and pies take flight,
In a feast of smiles, we eat with delight.

The table's set, a carnival spread,
Oops! My soup just landed on Fred!
With every bite, another joke,
In this gathering, happiness spoke.

We pass the bread, and then the wine,
Each clink of glasses feels just divine.
Who knew that crumbs could be so grand?
In this merry chaos, together we stand.

So grab a fork, make some room,
A side of laughter, and culinary boom!
With each shared dish, our hearts entwine,
In the humor of sharing, we all feel fine.

The Path of Selflessness

In a world wide as a pizza pie,
It's nice to know, no one should cry.
With open hearts and silly hats,
We strut together, like laughter-spats!

On this path, we trip and fall,
But hey, isn't that the fun of it all?
We share our duds, and some old socks,
"Here, take my coat!
"I'll borrow your crocs!"

With giggles bubbling like freshly popped corn,
We help each other without a frown.
And when you lend me your elbow grease,
Together we grin with overwhelming peace!

So dance along this goofy lane,
Where kindness flows like, well... outrageous gain.
Let's tumble forth, laughing loud,
On this wild path, we'll share our proud.

Voices of Generosity

In the town square, everyone sings,
With voices loud, and very funny things.
"Hey, my friend, take this old shoe,
It may seem weird, but it's just for you!"

A dog barks back, "What's all this fuss?
When's it my turn? I'm full of trust!"
With wagging tails and a chorus loud,
We give and share, feeling quite proud.

For every hug, a story is spun,
And each silly act has a double-fun!
Like gifts exchanged by friends in a line,
With chuckles and chuckles, our hearts align.

So let's raise our voices to the sky,
With a howling tune, oh my, oh my!
The world's a stage of laughter and cheer,
In this funny act, we shed every fear.

Kindred Spirits

In the dance of joy, we twirl and sway,
Each step we take feels like play.
With jokes that bounce like rubber balls,
We chase down giggles through friendly halls.

Our hearts are tied with silly string,
In this madcap world, we let laughter ring.
We trade our quirks like baseball cards,
With a wink and nudge, we play our parts.

Like peanut butter and jelly we pair,
Sharing secrets and antics beyond compare!
So come on in, the door is wide,
With kindred spirits, we take pride.

Let's sprinkle joy like confetti in the air,
In this carnival of kindness, we're debonair.
With every laugh, our souls unite,
In this zany dance of sheer delight.

Unseen Hands at Work

In the kitchen, pots clash and clang,
A sneaky chef, with a spatula, sang.
Gravy spills, and flour takes flight,
What a sight, oh what a delight!

Gifts of cookies, wrapped with care,
But half of them vanished, where?
Under the bed or in a hat,
Oh, the joy of sharing, how about that?

A card in my mailbox, how sweet and kind,
But the prankster's smile was hard to find.
It's all in good jest, we laugh and we play,
Life's greatest treasures? They simply go astray!

So here's to the chaos, the laughter, the cheer,
For giving and giggles, we hold most dear.
In the wacky world of friends and delight,
Every mishap becomes a joyful sight!

A Whisper of Altruism

A whisper slipped out from behind the couch,
"Could you spare some peanuts?" asked a mouse.
With a twitch of his nose and a grin on his face,
He's the sneakiest giver in this crowded space!

A cat on the prowl, with intentions so sly,
"Sharing is caring?" he gave it a try.
He knocked over snacks, as he danced in a jig,
Soon the party was huge, a crowd so big!

The goldfish, in front of the cake on the ledge,
Considered swimming far, near the hedge.
With a flip of his tail, he spread joy like seeds,
Turning every disaster to hilarious deeds!

So in this merry mayhem, we find our way,
Through laughter and joy, we brighten the day.
A whisper of kindness, it carries us high,
With giggles like bubbles, and spirits that fly!

Stars of Benevolence

Under the stars, with gifts piled high,
A raccoon was plotting, oh my, oh my!
With a twinkle and wink, he'd already begun,
Taking treats from the pantry, just for some fun!

A squirrel in mittens, so happy and spry,
Took the garland all wrapped, on the sly.
"Let's deck the halls," he cheerfully chirped,
While the humans below, just awkwardly burped!

A gleam in the night, a dance on the lawn,
These stars of goodwill? They've happily drawn,
With bated breath, they're all waiting to see,
What happens next, oh what will it be?

In the end, it's abundance, with giggles and cheer,
Sharing our laughter, we hold so dear.
For kindness is funny, from cats to the mice,
In this wild, wacky world, it all feels so nice!

Seeds of Selflessness

In a garden of giggles, the seeds start to sprout,
With each little bloom, there's laughter throughout.
The bees buzzed along, making honey with glee,
While teasing the flowers, "You're pranking for free!"

A squirrel took notes, in a tiny green book,
On how to make mischief, oh, take a good look!
"Sharing is fun," he scribbled in a rush,
Then dropped his acorn with a most hilarious hush!

Raindrops fell gently, like laughter in air,
Each splash was a chuckle, without a care.
We water the joy, with smiles we sow,
For funny little moments, in kindness we grow!

So let's plant our hearts, with humor and grace,
In this garden of nonsense, we all find our place.
For healing and laughter go hand in hand,
In the fertile soil of a giving land!

The Warm Embrace

When I found a sweater too large for me,
I thought of my neighbor who loved a good spree.
In a closet it sat, gathering much dust,
Until I freed it with laughter and trust.

Wrapped in wool, she looked quite a sight,
Hoping she'd wear it, she'd strut with delight.
So I gave it away, feeling so spry,
Now she says she's a fashionista—oh my!

And the mittens? They're a mystery for sure,
They fit an octopus—this I endure!
But at least there's warmth in every cold breeze,
With laughter and giggles, and moments to seize.

So here's to the sweater that warmed us both bright,
While neighbors keep sharing and spreading pure light.
A tale of a closet, a laugh, and some cheer,
In giving, we gather, the fun's always near!

Radiance in the Darkness

A flashlight I found on a shelf collecting dust,
I called my friend Joe—"Hey, this is a must!"
He said with a chuckle, his voice quite a blast,
"Great! Now I can find my lost sandwich at last!"

When the power went out, Joe lit up the block,
With a party of snacks, who knew he could rock?
His glow worm enthusiasm really took flight,
He danced 'neath the ceiling, a truly bright sight!

So the flashlight went blurry, but laughter stayed strong,
We played charades while the darkness went long.
In the chaos of fun, we forgot all the fright,
Who needs a lamp when your friends are the light?

So here's to the darkness that brought out the glee,
And to Joe with his snacks, a friend meant to be.
With radiance and laughter, we'll forever recall,
How fun in the dark can brighten it all!

Baskets of Hope

At the market one day, I spied a big basket,
Filled with odd fruits; oh, what a great casket!
"Banana or llama?" I pondered with glee,
I decided to share it with friends over tea.

We laughed at the pears that looked oddly round,
Discussing the best way to make a sound.
"Let's open a fruit stand!" cried out silly Sue,
"But with these funny shapes, what can we do?"

We made fruit hats, and danced to our tune,
Wearing pineapples shaped like the moon.
So out went the baskets filled with delight,
Our market stand thrived 'neath friendly moonlight!

With laughter as seasoning and cheer in each bite,
Those fruits once forgotten brought pure, silly light.
So the baskets of hope became treasures anew,
In sharing and laughter, a funny crew grew!

Currents of Care

On a windy day, with kites in the air,
I lent out my kite to a girl with bright hair.
She laughed as it soared, then it snagged on a tree,
"Oops!" cried my kite, "Looks like I'm stuck, whee!"

We stood there in giggles, watching it sway,
Her mom threw a snack—yummy treats in the fray!
So we sat on the grass, devising a plan,
To rescue my poor kite, that mischievous man!

With a pizza cutter, a broom, and some string,
We conquered the height like we were the king!
At last, my kite landed with grace in our midst,
Presenting a snack festival, who could resist?

So here's to the laughs in the midst of a care,
To kites and to snacks, and adventures to share.
In sharing our moments, we find something rare,
Currents of joy flow through love when we dare!

Flourishing Hearts

A pie for the dog, what a curious sight,
He danced on two legs with delight!
Giving is easy, just look around,
Even the cat came, it had to be found.

Throwing socks in a box, what a delight,
A party for mismatches, let's party all night!
Neighbors all laughing, it's quite the affair,
Sharing odd socks, with nary a care.

Pasta for breakfast, who would have guessed?
A lunch for the squirrels, now that's a true test!
The fun isn't just in the food that we share,
It's the giggles and joy floating through air.

So grab a cupcake, let laughter abound,
In this banquet of friendship, joy can be found!
With each silly gesture, more hearts entwine,
Together we flourish, how truly divine!

In the Footsteps of Altruism

An old man with chimes, oh what a sound,
He jingles with glee, spinning round and round!
Offering laughter with each little grin,
He brings joy like gifts, where do we begin?

The kids skateboarding, all tangled in glee,
They share their last cookie, just need one, you see?
Running in circles, they giggle and shout,
Helping each other, no shadows of doubt.

A neighbor who bakes, oh what a fine treat,
Muffins and donuts, can't resist that sweet!
They toss them like confetti, oh what a fun sight,
Spreading joy everywhere, it feels so right.

In these moments of laughter, we see it's all true,
That sharing is caring, it's best for the crew!
With each little chuckle, a bond starts to form,
A wacky wild world where kindness is born!

Wings of Generosity

A bird on a bike, how peculiar, it seems,
Delivering goodies to all of our dreams!
With gifts in its beak and a wink in its eye,
It zooms through the sky, oh my, oh my!

A cat in a hat, playing Santa it seems,
Clumsily stumbling, fulfilling our dreams.
It's not just the gifts that make our hearts sing,
It's the laughter and joy that together we bring.

With aprons and spoons, the kitchen's a mess,
Baking odd treats, no need to impress!
Flour on our noses, we dance all about,
Spreading some kindness, that's what it's about!

So come join the fun, here's a seat next to me,
With goofy companions, so wild and free.
From silly to sweet, let the joy take its flight,
In this wacky world, everything feels right!

Sparks of Unity

A jug filled with laughter, let it overflow,
With jokes and some tickles, who doesn't love a show?
From wacky wild dances to silly balloon fights,
We spark up the fun on those long winter nights.

With cookies and cupcakes, our tower is great,
Sharing our desserts, oh don't be late!
Mismatched our spoons, but we all take a bite,
In our joyful chaos, everything feels right.

From swing sets to laughter, we build quite the tower,
A wild concoction, bringing unity power!
Together we tangle, in this grand jubilee,
Creating a world that's as fun as can be!

So let's toss confetti and sing all the tunes,
Create a grand celebration beneath the bright moons!
With every sweet moment, we find our delight,
In the laughter we share, our spirits take flight!

The Light We Carry

In a world so bright, we dress in cheer,
Spreading giggles far and near.
Like a madman with a box of cats,
We share our snacks, and all that spats!

With oversized bows on heads we wear,
We gift our friends outrageous flair.
Like pineapples dressed in a tutu,
We hope these gifts will amuse you too!

Rolling presents down the hall,
Wrapped in laughter, we have a ball.
Like clowns juggling pies and dreams,
Our gifts bring joy, or so it seems!

In the end, it's all about glee,
Like ice cream cones from a bumblebee.
So let's spread fun, not a frown,
With goofy antics, we'll wear the crown!

Waves of Generosity

Surfing the tide of fun galore,
We ride on waves to the sandy shore.
With buckets of joy, we build sand castles,
Throw in some laughter, and spirit dazzles!

Like seagulls fighting for a fry,
We share our treats, oh my, oh my!
Tossing jellybeans in the air,
We cheer, 'Hey, look! A sugar bear!'

In beach towels wrapped, we giggle and grin,
Like dolphins leaping, we spin and spin.
With flip-flops flapping, we run and chase,
Handing out smiles at a lightning pace!

As sunset glows, laughter takes flight,
Our hearts like kites dancing in sight.
So let's catch waves of silly delight,
And spread our joy until the night!

Gifts of the Heart

With boxes bursting at the seams,
We wrap our wishes with silly themes.
Like penguins in tuxedos strut,
We deliver joy with each little cut!

A rubber chicken here, a whoopee cushion there,
A heartfelt giggle, we love to share.
With tinsel tangled in hair just right,
Our gifts bring sparkles to the night!

We trade our socks and mismatched shoes,
Draw the line at bad dance moves.
Like kittens stuck in a yarn, we play,
Giggles erupt on this crazy day!

So here's to laughter, the best kind of art,
Wrapped up in joy, the gifts from the heart.
With each crazy gift, a story's found,
In the humor of giving, our love's profound!

Beneath Open Arms

Under the sky with arms stretched wide,
We offer hugs like a bumpy ride.
Wearing sweaters two sizes too small,
We cuddle close, not caring at all!

With cupcakes topped in rainbow sprinkles,
We share the joy; it makes toes tingle.
Like squirrels hoarding acorns galore,
Our laughter spills out, we want to explore!

In giant shoes, we leap and bound,
Crafting giggles that circle around.
With hearts like balloons, and voices that sing,
Together we spread the joy that we bring!

So let's gather 'round, oh what a scene,
With hands full of kindness, if you know what I mean.
In this wild dance, let's play our part,
For beneath open arms, we nurture the heart!

Echoes of Generosity

A squirrel with acorns stashed away,
Dodging a cat who's come out to play.
He offers a nut to a startled dove,
Squeaking, "Here's a treat, it's made with love!"

A child shares her cookie in a grand way,
To the boy next door who forgot his whey.
He grins with a face now smudged with crumbs,
"I'll trade you for kindness, or maybe some drums!"

A dragon in town with a heart full of mirth,
Gives out fireflies for joy and for girth.
"Catch one or two, they glow bright at night,
But watch out for sadness that takes off in flight!"

A goat in a sweater decides to lend,
His warm woolly goodness as a soft trend.
"Wear my coat, dear friend, let's frolic and cheer,
And spread all this warmth 'til winter draws near!"

A Heart Open Wide

A penguin with gifts that just don't quite fit,
Gives socks to a seal who can't stand the wit.
He slips on the socks and gives them a twirl,
"These are quite fancy, let's dance, give it a whirl!"

A bear shares his honey with a buzzing bee,
"What's sweet on my plate, well, that's fine with me!"
The bee rolls his eyes, oh what a delight,
"Do you know your honey is sticky and bright?"

An octopus juggles some pink jellyfish,
Offering colors, one quirky wish.
"Here's some fun, take two if you dare,
And let's paint the ocean, I'll catch you a chair!"

A fox with a hat that's too big for his head,
Gives it to a rabbit, he's better off instead.
"Let's prance in this hat, and look quite absurd,
While we tumble and roll, oh haven't you heard?"

Threads of Kindness

A cat with a yarn ball, oh what a surprise,
Starts knitting a sweater for all of her ties.
"This one's for you and this one's for me,
Let's match in our style and dance with glee!"

A turtle comes by, all slow and grand,
Offers some sunshine and a soft, warm hand.
"Let's weave our tales with laughter and fun,
I'll take my time, you can zoom and I'll run!"

A parrot who squawks and shares all her tunes,
Hands out some rhythm beneath lovely moons.
"Sing loud with me, let's cause a ruckus,
In the jungle of joy, we'll create such a fuss!"

A rabbit hops in, with lettuce to spare,
Sharing a snack with a feathered affair.
"You get the greens, I'll take the bright red,
Together we'll munch and hop straight to bed!"

Gifts of the Mind

A wizard named Fred with a silly old hat,
Decides to share knowledge, imagine that!
"With every spell cast, I'll teach you a rhyme,
But first, let's cha-cha 'til the end of time!"

A robot named Benny, with circuits galore,
Programmed to dance when he finds a door.
"Let's trade some moves and turn up the beat,
While servers of laughter serve up a treat!"

A fish with a wish writes tales on the flow,
Sharing great stories of where they all go.
"Travel with me through the bubbles 'n swish,
And let's make a wave, what a grand fishy wish!"

A raccoon with glasses, wise as can be,
Gives lessons on scavenging, come see!
"Let's find the good stuff, it's scattered around,
With smarts and some giggles, let's have fun abound!"

Acts of Silent Sacrifice

A bird dropped crumbs on my neighbor's lawn,
While I was busy munching a scone.
She chased the thief, oh what a scene,
But the bird just squawked, 'I'm no food machine!'

In a meeting, I lent my pen,
Not knowing it was a prized fountain gem.
The look on their face was quite the delight,
As they whispered, 'This pen's outta sight!'

Old socks I donated with care,
They said they'd keep me warm, or wear?
"To the dog park they go!" I claimed with a grin,
As they wrapped around a pup's wagging chin.

Gave my last cookie in a friendly duel,
But they offered me milk like a generous fool.
Now we share crumbs as we giggle and muse,
Sometimes sacrifice means a sweet sugar fuse.

The Lantern of Compassion

I lit a candle for a friend in need,
But the wax dripped low, oh what a deed!
It missed the plate and waxed the cat,
Now they're a fuzzy, drippy aristocrat!

A neighbor's light bulb went bang in the night,
So I gave them mine, oh what a plight!
In the dark, we giggled with flashlights in hand,
Pretending to be a ghostly dance band.

When I found some change under my chair,
I tossed it in a jar, with minimal care.
Turns out it held wisdom, along with the coin,
'To be rich in laughter is what we must join!'

Baked a pie for the bake sale galore,
But forgot the sugar and opened a door.
Now it's a "mystery" pie, such tasty delight,
Wondering who'd dare take a bite on that night!

A Haven of Hope

There's a box on my porch, all wrapped in gold,
Thought it was treasure, or stories untold.
But it was more socks, quite the surprise,
Now I'm swathed in colors that surely defy!

Mom said, "Help people, arrange these chairs,"
So I made a fort, filled with some snares.
When they sat down and the chairs went boom,
We all laughed and forgot the gloom.

A friend lost a pet, so I bought her a toy,
It squeaked a song, oh what joy!
But it startled the dog, made a wild race,
Barking in tune, it joined in the chase!

Every heart has a minute or two to share,
And laughter often finds us hiding somewhere.
Let's unwrap kindness with giggles and cheer,
When giving our all brings happiness near.

Kindness in the Air

I tried to be nice, gave my umbrella away,
To a neighbor caught in a sunny downpour's play.
They laughed and just shrugged, with a smile so wide,
Said, "I'd rather get wet than be stuck here inside!"

A squirrel stole my lunch, what a nerve!
I chased him around, oh, how I swerved!
He shared it with friends, now they're living large,
In a nutty café, they're running a charge!

I offered my car for a ride to the fest,
Thought it'd be fun, how I jest!
But my tires sang songs like a childish choir,
So, we danced to the tune, putting hearts in our fire.

Little deeds blossom like daisies in spring,
With chuckles and joy, feel the happiness ring.
So toss a kind word into the open air,
And watch as it twirls, spreading laughter everywhere!

Light in Every Gesture

In a world where socks go missing,
I donate my last pair, quite dismissing.
Not a fashion trend or style I seek,
But a laugh at my own barefooted streak.

Handing out treats, it's a sugar rush,
With jelly beans tossed in a wild hush.
Brightening faces as candy does fly,
Like confetti, I let the sweet moments sigh.

My cat's on a diet, but here's dry food,
I just hope it doesn't lower the mood.
With a wink and a grin thrown their way,
I share while they plot for their heist every day.

Remember, a giggle can lighten the load,
A candy bar shared brightens an old road.
With jokes in the packet and joy on the side,
Those small, silly gifts spread laughter worldwide.

The Warmth of Your Hands

When winter arrives, I knit hats by the dozen,
Though they look like hats made for a fuzzy cousin.
Each stitch is a giggle, each loop a delight,
I'm gifting warm chaos to make spirits bright.

In my kitchen, I bake cookies so round,
Though some end up square – that's flavor unbound!
With sprinkles like confetti, I serve them with cheer,
As friends roll their eyes but keep coming near.

A warm cup of cocoa shared with a grin,
I'll float a marshmallow on top of my kin.
But beware of the whimsy, it'll stick like glue,
You'll find cocoa rivers in places quite new.

With laughter and warmth, we hold hands and sing,
As stories and chocolate make our hearts take wing.
The warmth that flows from a mug or a jest,
Is a gift that ignites, and it gives us the best.

Seeds of Compassion

I plant little seeds in a garden so wide,
With carrots that giggle and peas that abide.
When they sprout little faces, I'm taken aback,
Could these veggies be plotting a cheeky attack?

Around the neighborhood, I spread bread that's old,
To squirrels in suits, it's a sight to behold!
Chewing and chattering, they gather with glee,
While I chuckle a bit at the nutty degree.

Each furrow I make has a tale of its own,
Like sharing my toys, even when I'm alone.
For laughter is rooted in kindness that grows,
And humor, like flowers, always overflows.

A sprinkle of joy in each gesture we share,
Is the magic that dances in love everywhere.
It's a harvest of giggles we tend and we sow,
With seeds of compassion that help friendships grow.

A Tapestry of Hope

In the midst of chaos, I thread some bright yarn,
A tapestry of laughter to decorate the barn.
Strands of my silliness woven with flair,
A patchwork of bright smiles hangs high in the air.

I gift silly socks, mismatched with intent,
Feet in bright colors, I proudly lament.
Last week's fashion statement? A dazzling sight,
For laughter's the fabric that keeps us all tight.

With crayons and laughter, I draw out a plan,
To brighten the day with a wacky canvas span.
Each humor-filled stroke, adding joy, oh so grand,
Filling the corners of hearts across the land.

So let's stitch together our whims and our cheers,
In a world where kindness could drown out the fears.
For hope is a tapestry, spun with a grin,
A quilt of our laughter that warms from within.

The Gift of Listening

In a room full of chatter, I nod and I grin,
But half of the time, I think of my gin.
They share their deep secrets, I giggle and sway,
Just give me a snack, and I'm happy to stay.

I hear all their woes while I munch on a fry,
They spill all their thoughts, like bees in the sky.
I nod like a puppet, though I've lost the thread,
Inside I'm just plotting the next meal instead.

Each tale that they tell goes in one ear and out,
While I plan my escape with a laugh and a pout.
Their sorrows, like cake, I sure hope they won't slice,
For sharing's a joy, but I'd prefer it with ice.

So talk all you want, I won't mind, oh dear,
Just know when it's over, I'll still want my beer.
With ears open wide, and a chuckle or two,
The gift of good listening... as long as it's stew.

The Dance of Generous Souls

Oh, let's all do the generosity sway,
Where I give you my snack and then dance it away!
We'll twirl with our kindness, two-step with our hearts,
While you borrow my fries, that's how friendship starts.

Spin me a tale of your last weekend trip,
While I share my last chip, just one savory dip.
With laughter as loud as a bouncing balloon,
The dance is contagious; we'll glide to the moon.

You take my last muffin; I'll swat at the flies,
We barter our snacks with light-hearted sighs.
A swirl and a twirl, then you take my last bite,
In the dance of the generous, everything's right!

So grab me a burger; let's waltz with our fries,
In this fun little shimmy, we'll share all our pies.
For giving is splendid, as we spin and we scoop,
In the dance of our laughter, let's form a big group!

Flames of Consideration

There's a fire crackling, it's hotter than me,
I toss in some goodwill, let it burn and be free!
With marshmallows of kindness, we roast them with glee,

The flames of compassion, they're roasting for three.

I pass you the s'mores, they're sticky and sweet,
But mark my words, buddy, I won't share my treat!
The flames dance around, they're merry and bright,
But under that glow, just don't steal my bite.

With laughter like smoke, curling up to the stars,
Each crackle of kindness strikes joy in our hearts.
The warmth of good deeds, it's a beautiful glow,
But I'll guard my snacks tightly; just thought you should know.

So let's stoke our own fires and keep them aglow,
We'll gather our friends, let the good vibes flow.
In the warmth of our whims, let's twirl with delight,
With flames of consideration, we'll party all night!

Echoes of Almsgiving

In a world filled with laughter, let's echo our cheer,
I'll give you my last donut; don't shed a tear!
The whims of my heart beats for sharing with you,
Even if donuts make my belt feel askew.

A dollar or two, it's a small, tiny fling,
While I'm here giving snacks, you can give me a ring.
With echoes of kindness that bounces around,
Let's spread all the giggles, let joy be unbound.

You take half my burger, I'll take half your fries,
A sharing extravaganza with silly surprise.
From pocket to pocket, let's pass all the treats,
In the echoes of giving, we dance on our feet.

So ring up your friends, let's gather for fun,
The echoes of kindness have only begun.
From laughter to munching, we'll fill up the day,
In a world full of joy, we'll dance all the way!

Moments of Grace

One day I bought a present, oh so sly,
Hid it in my closet, thought I'd let it fly.
But the dog found it first, unwrapped with glee,
Now he's dancing with ribbons, and it's all on me!

I thought I'd share my lunch, a tasty treat,
But my cat claimed it first, her purrs were sweet.
She licked my sandwich clean, left crumbs in the air,
Guess sharing's a skill, I need to prepare!

I gave my worn shoes to a friend so dear,
But he wore them out, now it's the end of the year.
He runs like the wind, in my old torn pair,
I guess kindness bites back; now I'm in despair!

Sometimes charity's funny, don't you see?
You give, you take back, it's all like a spree.
With laughter and mischief, it's all in the play,
Moments of grace in a wacky ballet!

Cradled in Kindness

A pie I baked for neighbors, oh such delight,
But my dog had a taste, it vanished from sight.
I knocked on their doors saying, "Is this a crime?"
They said, "Bring us more, it's a doggone good time!"

I knitted some mittens, a gift full of love,
But they fit my cat better, all fluffy and guv.
Now she struts 'round proudly, a feline so grand,
While I'm left mittless, the cold I'll withstand!

I tried to lend money, so my friend could have fun,
But he bought a rubber chicken and then he would run.
Now we've got clucks echoing through all the halls,
Who knew that kindness would lead to such calls?

So here's to our blunders, the mishaps we face,
In cradled compassion we find our own grace.
With laughter, we bounce back from each little fumble,
As kindness brings joy, and our giggles all tumble!

The Dance of Empathy

I loaned my friend a book, thought I'd be nice,
But now it's lost forever, like a roll of dice.
Instead, we share scraps of wisdom and cheese,
In our dance of goodwill, I'll take what I please!

A shirt that I gave him, oh, what a throw!
He wore it as a cape, put on quite a show.
Now he's off saving cats, with a grin ear to ear,
Empathy's a giggle, with style and cheer!

One day I baked cupcakes, they came out real weird,
Instead of sprinkles, I used what I feared.
"Just sprinkle on laughter!" said my friend with no stress,

Now they're known at the party as "Cupcakes in Mess!"

With every small gesture, we jump and we prance,
In the dance of compassion, we laugh and we dance.
Though our kindness is quirky, it brings joy each day,
The dance of empathy finds the funniest way!

Tides of Togetherness

We built a sandcastle, under the sun,
But it turned to a moat, with waves of fun.
Dressed like a crab, my friend slipped and fell,
Now we're the lords of a soggy sand shell!

At the beach, sharing snacks, what a delight!
But seagulls swooped down, it was quite a sight.
Our lunch went airborne, flying high in the blue,
Together we laughed, in our feathery zoo!

We found a lost flip-flop, it went on a trip,
So we held a summit, to chart its next zip.
The tides bring us close, with games made of foam,
In togetherness, these moments feel like home!

When laughter surrounds us, like shells on the shore,
In the tides of our friendship, we'll always explore.
With fun and mischief, and joy on display,
Together we'll sail, come what may!

The Light We Share

A candle flickers, bright and bold,
With wicks so short, it's getting old.
We pass it round, like a hot potato,
'It's your turn now!' we gleefully shout.

In a room so dark, it starts to sing,
With laughter loud, oh what joy we bring!
But careful now, don't knock it over,
Or we'll all be left to hover!

Sharing snacks like it's a prize,
One last cookie, oh, what a surprise!
We trade and giggle, like little kids,
Guilty grins over all that we did.

So here's a toast, with lemonade,
To those who give, and never afraid.
May our light shine, unabashed and true,
And bring us laughter, like a big debut!

Embracing Abundance

In a world where bananas grow taller than trees,
We find ourselves laughing with utmost ease.
The fruit flies in, but we're all on guard,
'That's my banana!' each one says hard.

With every meal, we mix and match,
A salad of flavors, watch our hearts hatch.
"Try this!" we say, "I've added some spice!"
But wait, is that cheese? "Oh, that'll be nice!"

We'll fill our plates like they're our dreams,
Pasta for days, or so it seems.
And when the feasting finally ends,
We save leftovers for our dear friends.

So let's raise a toast, to this quirky feast,
With laughter and joy, we're never least.
In a world of plenty, we all take part,
With belly laughs, and an open heart!

A Symphony of Giving

The band strikes up, out of tune and giddy,
Notes fly around; oh boy, that's pretty!
"Play it again!" we all keenly shout,
But soon the rhythm goes sideways, no doubt.

A horn blows loud, and the drums go boom,
A cacophony fills up the room!
But we smile and dance, even if it's wrong,
For music is magic, it makes us belong.

As we pass the baton, what a sight to see,
One plays the kazoo, another on a bee!
We gather the notes, as if they were gold,
Every laugh shared, a story retold.

In our grand orchestra of heart and cheer,
We harmonize joy, wipe away each tear.
So let's play together, one raucous refrain,
With laughter our score, we'll dance in the rain!

Footprints of Kindness

Through muddy paths, we forward march,
With squishy shoes, that become quite a starch.
Let's leave some prints, not just in the mud,
A smile in each step, then we'll clean off the crud.

Stomp, hop, skip, what a messy delight,
Our footprints combined, funny and bright.
Oh look, a heart! Who drew that so grand?
Only to slip, now we're hand in hand!

We'll leave trails of giggles, tie-dye and fun,
Group hugs and laughter, everyone's won!
So follow our paths, they twist and they bend,
In the footprints of kindness, we're all just pretend.

With every splash, we splash in delight,
Embracing the silliness, hearts feeling light.
So come take a stroll, through joy that we find,
In each little step, we share what's so kind.